ADAPTABILITY
Maximizing Change

Newton Elikem Kwashie

Introduction

Many changes and new conditions arise out of foreseen and unforeseen circumstances.

The Coronavirus-19 (SARS COV-2) came at a point where human beings did not prepare for it. No change comes announced. It caused a lot of shifts and twists to human life and existence.

This pandemic ravished and spread throughout the world at a fast rate. No country was spared. All the countries of the world have cases of COVID-19.

When the signs of COVID-19 started in 2019 in the city of Wuhan in China, the world did less to control it.

This pandemic has taken more lives and destroyed most of the world's economies if not all. Sophisticated countries could not control it.

The pandemic came and made things bare. Many system failures were exposed by the pandemic. Systems and structures which were faulty and deceptive to be strong but were weak and not worthy of the praise we gave them. The virus was timely in testing systems and structures of organizations and institutions.

Safety protocols like washing of hands under running water with soap, application of hand sanitizer, and compulsory wearing of a nose mask. Governments introduced these protocols to control the spread of the virus.

Governments were under pressure. It was not attractive to be president and head of state at the period. Lockdowns and restrictions were introduced. Governments and private individuals offered food, money, and other social interventions to support citizens.

The pandemic threatened human existence, but through it all, we survived and sailed through. We give glory to God for keeping us by His mercy and love. We pay respect to all who died and people who risked their lives at the frontline of the battle (frontline health workers and security agencies). It has become one of the normal diseases and infections in the world now.

Why all this long flashback and history? I came to let you understand this pandemic was a major change that distorted the way of doing things across the globe.

Events, services, governments, and other aspects of the economies were truncated. Crowds were locked out of events centres, stadia, church auditoriums, etc. The only people who were allowed to be out there were essential workers like health workers, and security agencies, among others.

This change led to innovations and inventions: we had to devise ways and methods of surviving the new norm – *adaptability*.

Adaptability can be said to be the ability to change or be changed to fit changed circumstances.

We must note that change is constant and we must develop the adaptation to suit those changes or new circumstances.

There are times as workers, Christians, and leaders, we are met with situations where we must strategize to fit into the new season.

We shall start this book with a chapter that talks about knowing that change is constant.

1

Know That Change Is Constant

Everything changes. Change in the world is constant. Our knowledge of the fact that times and seasons change is very important for survival. Knowledge is key in everything. Adaptability is very necessary because change is constant. Times and seasons change. Everything in this world changes, so expect change anytime. Know this and plan for it. God is the only constant in the universe.

There are various kinds of change we always have at our hands to work at. The changes vary from place to place and from time to time. There are physical, geographical, demographic, financial, health, and spiritual changes, among others.

God and our Lord Jesus Christ are just the two people that do not change. All people and things change and are bound to change.

God, the Creator of the universe and the Lord of hosts has remained the same from times past. He is not a man that is why He cannot change.

6 *For I am the LORD, I change not; therefore ye sons of Jacob are not consumed.*

Malachi 3:6

Our Lord Jesus Christ has remained the same from time past, is still the same, and does not intend to change any day and any time.

8 *Jesus Christ the same yesterday, and to day, and for ever.*

Hebrews 13:8

The writer of the Book of Ecclesiastes stated categorically that change is constant.

1 *To everything there is a season, and a time to every purpose under the heaven:*

2 *A time to be born, and a time to die; a time to plant, and a time to pluck up that which is planted;*

3 *A time to kill, and a time to heal; a time to break down,*
and a time to build up;

4 *A time to weep, and a time to laugh; a time to mourn,*
and a time to dance;

5 *A time to cast away stones, and a time to gather stones*
together; a time to embrace, and a time to refrain from
embracing;

6 *A time to get, and a time to lose; a time to keep, and a*
time to cast away;

7 A time to rend, and a time to sew; a time to keep
silence, and a time to speak;

8 *A time to love, and a time to hate; a time of war, and a*
time of peace.

9 *What profit hath he that worketh in that wherein he*
laboureth?

10 *I have seen the travail, which God hath given to the*
sons of men to be exercised in it.

Ecclesiastes 3:1-10

We are to know that before we learn to adapt, change is constant and this fact must guide you as you move about. As far as the earth remains and gravity is in motion, change is inevitable. There are times and seasons. These times and changes come for a purpose, and we must make them count.

We have to be prepared with a mentality to win and survive in those times and seasons and how we achieve that is determined by our perception. **Perception is the right spirit in which we move in challenging times.**

2

Perception

How you survive or the will to change to fit and be able to go about the season of change must first start with having the right perception.

Perception is the way of conceiving something. It is also noticing something and how to deal with it.

As believers, our perception of problems and challenges must be positive. You need the winner's mentality. We fight and face the challenges of this life from the point of victory and not a defeatist point of view.

The Bible states all things work together for the good of those who are called according to His purpose.

28 *And we know that all things work together for good to them that love God, to them who are the called according to his purpose.* *Romans 8:28*

Joseph was sold into slavery by his biological brothers. He was surprised and worried at the actions of his brothers' but his perception of the situation enthused him.

20 *But as for you, ye thought evil against me; but God meant it unto good, to bring to pass, as it is this day, to save much people alive.* *Genesis 50:20*

We must know and understand that if we are going to come out or rise from a circumstance, the mindset we carry about it matters.

God is a God of possibilities. Nothing is too hard for Him.

26 *But Jesus beheld them, and said unto them, With men this is impossible; but with God all things are possible.*

Matthew 19:26

We need to have a clear perception. Understanding boosts perception. To face a fresh change or situation that presents itself to us, we have to develop optimism.

The mentality of positivity, profit, and possibility should be the motive. The ability to rise and benefit from every challenge matters. Until you develop the right perception, you can never embrace new challenges and make the best of them.

Developing the right perception for survival and thriving should be our aim and focus when change comes.

Living things like a frog and other creatures which are amphibians can survive on land and water because of their abilities to adapt. They accept the change. They understand that change in environment is possible and conditions change, so they must learn to adapt to stay on land and in water when the need arises.

Paul the apostle was being transported to go face judgment when their ship was hard hit by a Euroclydon. Paul's perception helped to prevail over the circumstances. His fellow sailors were afraid and envisioned harm, but Paul was assured by the angel of the Lord's word.

1 *And when it was determined that we should sail into*
Italy, they delivered Paul and certain other prisoners
unto one named Julius, a centurion of Augustus' band.
2 *And entering into a ship of Adramyttium, we launched,*
meaning to sail by the coasts of Asia; one Aristarchus, a
Macedonian of Thessalonica, being with us.
3 *And the next day we touched at Sidon. And Julius*
courteously entreated Paul, and gave him liberty to go
unto his friends to refresh himself.
4 *And when we had launched from thence, we sailed*
under Cyprus, because the winds were contrary.
5 *And when we had sailed over the sea of Cilicia and*
Pamphylia, we came to Myra, a city of Lycia.
6 *And there the centurion found a ship of Alexandria*
sailing into Italy; and he put us therein.
7 *And when we had sailed slowly many days, and scarce*
were come over against Cnidus, the wind not suffering
us, we sailed under Crete, over against Salmone;

8 *And, hardly passing it, came unto a place which is*
called The fair havens; nigh whereunto was the city of
Lasea.
9 *Now when much time was spent, and when sailing was*
now dangerous, because the fast was now already past,
Paul admonished them,
10 *And said unto them, Sirs, I perceive that this voyage*
will be with hurt and much damage, not only of the
lading and ship, but also of our lives.
11 *Nevertheless the centurion believed the master and*
the owner of the ship, more than those things which were
spoken by Paul.
12 *And because the haven was not commodious to winter*
in, the more part advised to depart thence also, if by any
means they might attain to Phenice, and there to winter;
which is an haven of Crete, and lieth toward the south
west and north west.
13 *And when the south wind blew softly, supposing that*
they had obtained their purpose, loosing thence, they
sailed close by Crete.

14 But not long after there arose against it a
tempestuous wind, called Euroclydon.
15 And when the ship was caught, and could not bear up
into the wind, we let her drive.
16 And running under a certain island which is called
Clauda, we had much work to come by the boat:
17 Which when they had taken up, they used helps,
undergirding the ship; and, fearing lest they should fall
into the quicksands, strake sail, and so were driven.
18 And we being exceedingly tossed with a tempest, the
next day they lightened the ship;
19 And the third day we cast out with our own hands the
tackling of the ship.
20 And when neither sun nor stars in many days
appeared, and no small tempest lay on us, all hope that
we should be saved was then taken away.
21 But after long abstinence Paul stood forth in the
midst of them, and said, Sirs, ye should have hearkened
unto me, and not have loosed from Crete, and to have
gained this harm and loss. 22 *And now I exhort you to be*

of good cheer: for there shall be no loss of any man's life
among you, but of the ship.
23 *For there stood by me this night the angel of God,*
whose I am, and whom I serve,
24 *Saying, Fear not, Paul; thou must be brought before*
Caesar: and, lo, God hath given thee all them that sail
with thee.
25 *Wherefore, sirs, be of good cheer: for I believe God,*
that it shall be even as it was told me.
26 *Howbeit we must be cast upon a certain island.*
27 *But when the fourteenth night was come, as we were*
driven up and down in Adria, about midnight the
shipmen deemed that they drew near to some country;
28 *And sounded, and found it twenty fathoms: and when*
they had gone a little further, they sounded again, and
found it fifteen fathoms.
29 *Then fearing lest we should have fallen upon rocks,*
they cast four anchors out of the stern, and wished for
the day.

30 And as the shipmen were about to flee out of the ship,
when they had let down the boat into the sea, under
colour as though they would have cast anchors out of the
foreship,
31 Paul said to the centurion and to the soldiers, Except
these abide in the ship, ye cannot be saved.
32 Then the soldiers cut off the ropes of the boat, and let
her fall off.
33 And while the day was coming on, Paul besought
them all to take meat, saying, This day is the fourteenth
day that ye have tarried and continued fasting, having
taken nothing.
34 Wherefore I pray you to take some meat: for this is
for your health: for there shall not an hair fall from the
head of any of you.
35 And when he had thus spoken, he took bread, and
gave thanks to God in presence of them all: and when he
had broken it, he began to eat.
36 Then were they all of good cheer, and they also took
some meat.

37 *And we were in all in the ship two hundred threescore and sixteen souls.*

38 *And when they had eaten enough, they lightened the ship, and cast out the wheat into the sea.*

39 *And when it was day, they knew not the land: but they discovered a certain creek with a shore, into the which they were minded, if it were possible, to thrust in the ship.*

40 *And when they had taken up the anchors, they committed themselves unto the sea, and loosed the rudder bands, and hoised up the mainsail to the wind, and made toward shore.*

41 *And falling into a place where two seas met, they ran the ship aground; and the forepart stuck fast, and remained unmoveable, but the hinder part was broken with the violence of the waves.*

42 *And the soldiers' counsel was to kill the prisoners, lest any of them should swim out, and escape.*

43 *But the centurion, willing to save Paul, kept them from their purpose; and commanded that they which*

could swim should cast themselves first into the sea, and
get to land:
44 *And the rest, some on boards, and some on broken*
pieces of the ship. And so it came to pass, that they
escaped all safe to land.

Acts 27:1-44

When you perceive things, your actions are prepared for the future.

The way you think of issues matters a lot. Think positive. See any change as a way to rise and make good impressions out of it.

3

Accept The Change

As we have already established that change is constant, and the need to develop the right perception of circumstances, we then need to accept the change.

Accepting the change is the mental factor aside from the perception. Accepting the change is the will to face the situation. The truth of the matter is that if you do not accept the change, you cannot move.

It is widely known that humans dislike change, but some changes are beneficial. It is difficult to change or accept change, but for the better, we must accept the change and make the best of it.

Stubbornness is the lack of discipline to accept change. The Prophet Samuel compared rebellion to witchcraft.

23 For rebellion is as the sin of witchcraft, and stubbornness is as iniquity and idolatry. Because thou hast rejected the word of the LORD, he hath also rejected thee from being king. - 1 Samuel 15:23

We must know that until the change is accepted, nothing can be done but resort to complaints and excuses.

You would have to stay resolute and resolved. **Those who do not resolve dissolve into nothingness.**

Resolving is accepting that the change has come and you will have to do something with the change.

You do not just sit and watch things go worst, but you have to make things work.

David and Saul had grudges, and this led to many feuds among them. David kept winning over Saul. This was because David was resolved and built to face such moments.

***1** Now there was long war between the house of Saul and the house of David: but David waxed stronger and stronger, and the house of Saul waxed weaker and weaker.* *2 Samuel 3:1*

David, right from his days in the bush to the battle with Goliath and in the Cave of Adullam. His resolve was out of years of experiences and encounters with wilder beasts which thickened his skin to face the hate and attack of Saul.

It is worth noting that we must embrace the changes that come our way. We must adapt to them with positivity.

The changes that occur will not leave us, but we may have to develop the needed attitude to face every challenge with much readiness and zeal.

With perseverance and the will to do, we can become winners and victorious.

After we accept the change and work all the best we ought to adapt, some lessons must be learned with every change that we encounter. The next chapter will deal with it.

4

Learning

Your ability to learn from the changing times and seasons tells how much wisdom you have.

Your refusal to learn from the experiences you go through shows who you are. A fool does not learn from anything he or she goes through.

There are many lessons we have to learn from the changes we adapt to. It is not just a matter of adapting, but we have to take cues from them.

It is enough to adapt and make the best out of the change, but we are to learn from the experiences.

The COVID-19 pandemic has swept many families, businesses, ministries, etc. off their feet. This is because governments, people, and human institutions refused to learn.

The pandemic came with many changes to human living. How weddings, crowds management, and meetings are organized has changed.

If you refuse to learn, you will not earn. The learning we must do is very necessary. In this life, we are to learn all the time, either consciously or unconsciously, planned and unplanned and structured or unstructured. **If you are not updated, you get outdated.** We need to **unlearn, relearn, and learn** in the daily routine of our lives in whatever we do or go through. **The day you stop learning, you start dying. The more you know, the more you grow.**

Many institutions learned proper management and data gathering from the pandemic. This pandemic intended for many things to change around us, wastage, profligacy, recklessness, etc.

If COVID -19 did not teach you a lesson (s) and you did not learn from it, even ten thousand professors will not change you.

The pandemic came to teach humankind that we should co-exist and love others. The pandemic tested our human love, systems, and faith. The lessons taught by this pandemic are both positive and negative. The negatives were not as much as the positives. We are talking and worried about the negative changes and lessons it taught us and not the excellent and moral lessons we could glean from the pandemic. I know many lost their lives, jobs, and livelihood among many others, but there are positive lessons we can and should pick from the pandemic.

It is quite amazing to see how human beings were quick to return to our old ways and past *normals* after the Covid-19 restrictions were lifted off countries, without them learning anything from it.

There were a thousand and one lessons and adaptations we had to learn from this pandemic, but some of us have made no amends. As the pandemic has ended or has capsized, many who did not learn from it will remain the same till another hit them.

The church was tested by the fire of COVID -19. The commitment, dedication, and faith of believers were tested. The pandemic scattered abroad our members. Their love for God and faith was tested.

Businesses, organizations and ministries which lacked proper evaluation and analysis mechanisms with the needed systems and structures to hold the pressure of the distortion of the pandemic perished and did not survive the shock.

The Babylonians in slavery did not change their faith, they learned to trust and obey God. Their ability to adapt caused them to excel and flourish in slavery.

The Hebrew brothers – **Abednego, Meshach, and Shadrach** learned to trust from their experience.

Daniel, after the encounter in the lion's den, taught us to have full hope and reliance on God no matter what.

Paul the apostle was a phenomenal man of God. He knew how to abound and abase by the things he went through. He said to the Philippians that he could do all things because he learnt to live in plenty and lack.

10 *But I rejoiced in the Lord greatly, that now at the last*
your care of me hath flourished again; wherein ye were
also careful, but ye lacked opportunity.
11 *Not that I speak in respect of want: for I have*
learned, in whatsoever state I am, therewith to be
content.
12 *I know both how to be abased, and I know how to*
abound: everywhere and in all things I am instructed
both to be full and to be hungry, both to abound and to
suffer need.
13 *I can do all things through Christ which*
strengtheneth me. *Philippians 4:10-13*

We have to learn discipline and hard work from our life activities. **Laziness is resting before you are tired.**

Going back to the COVID-19 pandemic, I have learnt discipline, time management, frugality, excellence, and adequate preparation for the future.

The son of God, Jesus Christ, learnt many things from the things He suffered. God intended Jesus would learn obedience from the changes on earth during his lifetime on earth.

8 *Though he were a Son, yet learned he obedience by the things which he suffered;* *Hebrews 5:8*

Jesus Christ's ability to learn from the change that came His way gave Him the qualification for His elevation and promotion.

5 *Let this mind be in you, which was also in Christ Jesus:*

6 *Who, being in the form of God, thought it not robbery to be equal with God:*

7 *But made himself of no reputation, and took upon him the form of a servant, and was made in the likeness of men:*

8 *And being found in fashion as a man, he humbled himself, and became obedient unto death, even the death of the cross.*

9 *Wherefore God also hath highly exalted him, and given him a name which is above every name:*

10 *That at the name of Jesus every knee should bow, of things in heaven, and things in earth, and things under the earth;*

11 *And that every tongue should confess that Jesus Christ is Lord, to the glory of God the Father.*

Philippians 2:5-11

We need to take advantage of the opportunities that come our way through the changes. Lessons are to be learnt.

Every lesson learnt must equally lead us to maximize the change that comes our way. I will dedicate the last chapter to looking at how we must maximize the change we experience as we adapt.

5
Maximize The Change

The word, maximize simply *means making the best use or the best out of everything we do.*

As a people of God, we are to make the best out of every incident or situation that comes our way.

All things work together for us. I believe there is no accidental change, but they are meant to make the best come out of us.

28 And we know that all things work together for good to them that love God, to them who are the called according to his purpose. *Romans 8:28*

The David and Goliath story is one to consider when we talk about maximizing change. The endurance and perception of him being a winner from the days in the back side of the desert through to the Cave of Adullam until his reign as king, David, always took and went for the best out of every situation or circumstance he encountered.

*1 Now the Philistines gathered together their armies to
battle, and were gathered together at Shochoh, which
belongeth to Judah, and pitched between Shochoh and
Azekah, in Ephesdammim.*
*2 And Saul and the men of Israel were gathered together,
and pitched by the valley of Elah, and set the battle in
array against the Philistines.*
*3 And the Philistines stood on a mountain on the one
side, and Israel stood on a mountain on the other side:
and there was a valley between them.*
*4 And there went out a champion out of the camp of the
Philistines, named Goliath, of Gath, whose height was
six cubits and a span.*
*5 And he had an helmet of brass upon his head, and he
was armed with a coat of mail; and the weight of the
coat was five thousand shekels of brass.*
*6 And he had greaves of brass upon his legs, and a target
of brass between his shoulders.*
*7 And the staff of his spear was like a weaver's beam;
and his spear's head weighed six hundred shekels of
iron: and one bearing a shield went before him.*

8 And he stood and cried unto the armies of Israel, and
said unto them, Why are ye come out to set your battle in
array? am not I a Philistine, and ye servants to Saul?
choose you a man for you, and let him come down to me.
9 If he be able to fight with me, and to kill me, then will
we be your servants: but if I prevail against him, and kill
him, then shall ye be our servants, and serve us.
10 And the Philistine said, I defy the armies of Israel this
day; give me a man, that we may fight together.
11 When Saul and all Israel heard those words of the
Philistine, they were dismayed, and greatly afraid.
12 Now David was the son of that Ephrathite of
Bethlehemjudah, whose name was Jesse; and he had
eight sons: and the man went among men for an old man
in the days of Saul.
13 And the three eldest sons of Jesse went and followed
Saul to the battle: and the names of his three sons that
went to the battle were Eliab the firstborn, and next unto
him Abinadab, and the third Shammah.
14 And David was the youngest: and the three eldest
followed Saul.

*15 But David went and returned from Saul to feed his
father's sheep at Bethlehem.
16 And the Philistine drew near morning and evening,
and presented himself forty days.
17 And Jesse said unto David his son, Take now for thy
brethren an ephah of this parched corn, and these ten
loaves, and run to the camp to thy brethren;
18 And carry these ten cheeses unto the captain of their
thousand, and look how thy brethren fare, and take their
pledge.
19 Now Saul, and they, and all the men of Israel, were in
the valley of Elah, fighting with the Philistines.
20 And David rose up early in the morning, and left the
sheep with a keeper, and took, and went, as Jesse had
commanded him; and he came to the trench, as the host
was going forth to the fight, and shouted for the battle.
21 For Israel and the Philistines had put the battle in
array, army against army.
22 And David left his carriage in the hand of the keeper
of the carriage, and ran into the army, and came and
saluted his brethren.*

23 *And as he talked with them, behold, there came up the champion, the Philistine of Gath, Goliath by name, out of the armies of the Philistines, and spake according to the same words: and David heard them.*
24 *And all the men of Israel, when they saw the man, fled from him, and were sore afraid.*
25 *And the men of Israel said, Have ye seen this man that is come up? surely to defy Israel is he come up: and it shall be, that the man who killeth him, the king will enrich him with great riches, and will give him his daughter, and make his father's house free in Israel.*
26 *And David spake to the men that stood by him, saying, What shall be done to the man that killeth this Philistine, and taketh away the reproach from Israel? for who is this uncircumcised Philistine, that he should defy the armies of the living God?*
27 *And the people answered him after this manner, saying, So shall it be done to the man that killeth him.*
28 *And Eliab his eldest brother heard when he spake unto the men; and Eliab's anger was kindled against David, and he said, Why camest thou down hither? and with whom hast thou left those few sheep in the wilderness? I*

know thy pride, and the naughtiness of thine heart; for thou art come down that thou mightest see the battle.
29 *And David said, What have I now done? Is there not a cause?*
30 *And he turned from him toward another, and spake after the same manner: and the people answered him again after the former manner.*
31 *And when the words were heard which David spake, they rehearsed them before Saul: and he sent for him.*
32 *And David said to Saul, Let no man's heart fail because of him; thy servant will go and fight with this Philistine.*
33 *And Saul said to David, Thou art not able to go against this Philistine to fight with him: for thou art but a youth, and he a man of war from his youth.*
34 *And David said unto Saul, Thy servant kept his father's sheep, and there came a lion, and a bear, and took a lamb out of the flock:*
35 *And I went out after him, and smote him, and delivered it out of his mouth: and when he arose against me, I caught him by his beard, and smote him, and slew him.*

36 Thy servant slew both the lion and the bear: and this
uncircumcised Philistine shall be as one of them, seeing
he hath defied the armies of the living God.
37 David said moreover, The LORD that delivered me
out of the paw of the lion, and out of the paw of the bear,
he will deliver me out of the hand of this Philistine. And
Saul said unto David, Go, and the LORD be with thee.
38 And Saul armed David with his armour, and he put an
helmet of brass upon his head; also he armed him with a
coat of mail.
39 And David girded his sword upon his armour, and he
assayed to go; for he had not proved it. And David said
unto Saul, I cannot go with these; for I have not proved
them. And David put them off him.
40 And he took his staff in his hand, and chose him five
smooth stones out of the brook, and put them in a
shepherd's bag which he had, even in a scrip; and his
sling was in his hand: and he drew near to the Philistine.
41 And the Philistine came on and drew near unto David;
and the man that bare the shield went before him.

42 *And when the Philistine looked about, and saw David,*
he disdained him: for he was but a youth, and ruddy, and
of a fair countenance.
43 *And the Philistine said unto David, Am I a dog, that*
thou comest to me with staves? And the Philistine cursed
David by his gods.
44 *And the Philistine said to David, Come to me, and I*
will give thy flesh unto the fowls of the air, and to the
beasts of the field.
45 *Then said David to the Philistine, Thou comest to me*
with a sword, and with a spear, and with a shield: but I
come to thee in the name of the LORD of hosts, the God
of the armies of Israel, whom thou hast defied.
46 *This day will the LORD deliver thee into mine hand;*
and I will smite thee, and take thine head from thee; and
I will give the carcases of the host of the Philistines this
day unto the fowls of the air, and to the wild beasts of the
earth; that all the earth may know that there is a God in
Israel.
47 *And all this assembly shall know that the LORD*
saveth not with sword and spear: for the battle is the
LORD'S, and he will give you into our hands.

48 *And it came to pass, when the Philistine arose, and*
came and drew nigh to meet David, that David hasted,
and ran toward the army to meet the Philistine.
49 *And David put his hand in his bag, and took thence a*
stone, and slang it, and smote the Philistine in his
forehead, that the stone sunk into his forehead; and he
fell upon his face to the earth.
50 *So David prevailed over the Philistine with a sling and*
with a stone, and smote the Philistine, and slew him; but
there was no sword in the hand of David.
51 *Therefore David ran, and stood upon the Philistine,*
and took his sword, and drew it out of the sheath thereof,
and slew him, and cut off his head therewith. And when
the Philistines saw their champion was dead, they fled.
52 *And the men of Israel and of Judah arose, and*
shouted, and pursued the Philistines, until thou come to
the valley, and to the gates of Ekron. And the wounded of
the Philistines fell down by the way to Shaaraim, even
unto Gath, and unto Ekron.
53 *And the children of Israel returned from chasing after*
the Philistines, and they spoiled their tents.

54 *And David took the head of the Philistine, and brought it to Jerusalem; but he put his armour in his tent.*
55 *And when Saul saw David go forth against the Philistine, he said unto Abner, the captain of the host, Abner, whose son is this youth? And Abner said, As thy soul liveth, O king, I cannot tell.*
56 *And the king said, Enquire thou whose son the stripling is.*
57 *And as David returned from the slaughter of the Philistine, Abner took him, and brought him before Saul with the head of the Philistine in his hand.*
58 *And Saul said to him, Whose son art thou, thou young man? And David answered, I am the son of thy servant Jesse the Bethlehemite.* *1 Samuel 17:1-58*

Those who will benefit in precarious times are those who know they have to adapt to fresh changes and make the best of things.

It is not for those who make excuses, but for those who have the readiness to go for the best of every moment that comes.

As I stated in a book of mine – **FEAR**, I spelt fear as, ***Face Everything And Rise***. When others ***Forget Everything And Run***, courageous people who are ready to take the bull by the horn are the people who are celebrated and remembered in the annals of history.

With perseverance, hard work and diligence, we can adapt. The will and urge to make it when others are failing and making excuses keeps you going, pressing and pursuing.

The people of God are to look at the possibility and positivity of the situations than the negativity and the many reasons why it cannot happen.

I always say, look at why it should be done, rather than the reasons why it cannot be.

The changes that come, as I said early on, come for a purpose and as such, we have to make the best out of the situation.

The COVID-19 pandemic came to distort many things in the world, but many people, businesses, and others have made the best out of the pandemic, whiles others fell away by the wayside.

The Church of Jesus Christ was also hard hit by the ravishes of the pandemic. We had to evaluate and revise our strategies to stay relevant at the times. Using technology was to our benefit. We used social media portals in the mass propagation of the Gospel of our Lord Jesus Christ. I believe the Gospel of Jesus Christ gained much more coverage in the COVID-19 pandemic than in the pre-COVID era. We maximized the changed and we are where we are today because of the willingness and readiness to make it work.

Companies and businesses cashed in and cashed out in the pandemic season. People were not privileged to go out, so delivery agencies and shipping lines maximized the opportunity and they were prosperous. Those who did not take advantage of the time to make a profit from the change are late to do so now.

Factories and industries that produced vaccines, *"veronica buckets"*, nose masks, hand sanitizers, and other things to help curtail and control the spread of the virus reaped and made more wealth from the pandemic. They saw the change as a platform for prosperity and not poverty.

The owner of Amazon, Jeff Bezos, made and became very rich during the time. He maximized the change and rose for the task and made the best of the season. As others complained and made excuses, he and many more people made the best out of the period.

The future is not to the strong but to those adaptable to change.

Do not die. You should not give up. Do not quit now. Do not throw in the towel. Maximize the change. You should go for the change. When you muster the change with your strategies of adaptability will help you rise.

There is promotion in adaptation. There is always a reward for those who are ready to bear the risk and rise. The people of God should not shy away from pursuing, overtaking, and surely, we will recover all.

[8] *And David enquired at the LORD, saying, Shall I pursue after this troop? shall I overtake them? And he answered him, Pursue: for thou shalt surely overtake them, and without fail recover all.* 1 Samuel 30:8

Make every moment count. Go for it. Don't just survive it. Thrive wherever you are placed. The seasons and times change, they happen for a purpose.

Don't just survive but thrive. Thriving is your ability to blossom, be fruitful, and flourish. Survival is important. You need a survival instinct and the right perception to stay afloat whenever you find yourself in uncharted waters. Survive your wilderness.

Let Brotherly Love Continue!!!

www.ingramcontent.com/pod-product-compliance
Lightning Source LLC
LaVergne TN
LVHW010510160826
845677LV00012B/2764

* 9 7 9 8 3 5 3 8 6 5 2 7 8 *